Text and photographs by
Wayne Lynch

Whose TAIL Is This?

WALRUS
BOOKS

For Aubrey, who was always there

Edited by Viola Funk
Photography by Wayne Lynch
Interior design by Warren Clark and
    Setareh Ashrafologhalai
Typesetting and illustrations by
    Setareh Ashrafologhalai

Printed in China

Library and Archives Canada Cataloguing in Publication

Lynch, Wayne
    Whose tail is this? / Wayne Lynch.

Includes index.
ISBN 978-1-77050-008-2

    1. Tail—Juvenile literature. I. Title.

QL950.6.L95 2010   j573.9'98   C2009-906414-6

The publisher acknowledges the financial support of the Canada Council for the Arts, the British Columbia Arts Council, and the Government of Canada through the Canada Book Fund (CBF). Whitecap Books also acknowledges the financial support of the Province of British Columbia through the Book Publishing Tax Credit.

Canada Council   Conseil des Arts
for the Arts   du Canada

BRITISH COLUMBIA
ARTS COUNCIL

10 11 12 13 14 5 4 3 2 1

Most wild animals have some kind of tail. We humans are quite unusual because we don't have any tail, not even a tiny one. Imagine if you had a tail. Would it be short or long? If you had a long tail, where would you put it? Imagine all the funny things you could do with a long tail!

Animals have tails of many different shapes and sizes. Some tails are fuzzy, others are scaly. An animal's tail can even look like a paddle or a caterpillar with stripes. Animals use their tails to help them swim, to hold on to branches, and sometimes to signal their babies. See if you can figure out who owns the tails in this book.

I hope you won't laugh at my small fuzzy tail. Even if I make my tail stand straight in the air it's still pretty small. Fortunately, I don't use my tail for anything important. I don't need a big bushy tail because my whole bottom is a pale brown color that other animals like myself can see from far away. When I run from danger, others can see me leaving and they can also escape.

Who am I?

 am an elk. The large antlers on my head tell you that I am a male elk, called a bull. I live in the western mountains of North America. In winter, when the snow is deep, I use my big front hooves to dig underneath for dried grasses and the other plants that I like to eat. When I'm really hungry I also use my front teeth to scrape the thin bark from trees.

Each year in early spring, a male elk's antlers fall off. He grows a completely new set, often bigger than before.

I swim by moving my tail up and down. That's different than fish, which usually sweep their tails from side to side. I use my tail to dive to the ocean bottom, where I search for tasty worms and eels. I also like to eat many different kinds of fish. When I swim, I make lots of noises—buzzes, clicks, whistles, pops, and groans. That's why sailors sometimes call me the sea canary.

Who am I?

I am a beluga whale, the only whale that is all white in color. I live in the cold waters of the Arctic.

Every summer I grow a fresh new skin. To scrape off my old skin I like to rub my body on sand or gravel. Hundreds of belugas may travel to the same shallow river to do this.

Newborn belugas are dark gray in color and don't turn completely white until they are 10 years old or more.

The tip of my short tail looks as if it were dipped in black ink. I am a type of cat that lives in the northern forests of Canada and Alaska. The black tip on my tail is like a flag. It helps my babies to follow me through the forest and over the snow. I have a thick coat of fur that keeps me warm in winter even when it is very cold.

Who am I?

I am a mother lynx. In summer, I hunt beavers, muskrats, squirrels, mice, and birds. In winter, rabbits are my favorite food. I have big furry feet that let me run on top of the snow without sinking and this helps me to catch the speedy rabbits. When hunting is very good I can raise as many as five kittens in a year.

Lynx communicate with one another by moving their ears around. The long black hair on the tips of their ears makes their ears easier to see.

When you see my scaly tail and body, I bet you think I am a lizard of some kind. If you look closely though you'll see there is hair around my legs. No lizard has hair. When I get scared I run as fast as I can through thick bushes. The thick scales on my body keep me from getting hurt and also make it hard for hungry foxes and bobcats to grab me with their teeth.

Who am I?

I am an armadillo and I live in the warm areas of the southern United States. My curious name comes from the Spanish language and means "little animal with armor." I use my strong claws to dig in the dirt and my long, narrow nose to sniff under leaves for ants, earthworms, spiders, beetles, and crickets. When I find something good to eat, I use my sticky tongue to gobble it up.

When armadillos are not searching for food, they hide inside a burrow they dig under the roots of a tree.

My curly tail may look like an elephant's trunk, but don't be fooled. I'm much smaller than an elephant. Actually I could hide in the airhole at the end of an elephant's trunk! I often wrap my tail around a branch like an extra foot to help me climb and keep my balance.

Who am I?

19

I am a special kind of lizard called a chameleon. I live on the tropical island of Madagascar along the coast of southern Africa. The color of my skin quickly changes to bright red or yellow if I get excited or scared. At other times when I am relaxed and quiet, the color of my skin is brown or green to match the color of the bushes where I like to hide and hunt.

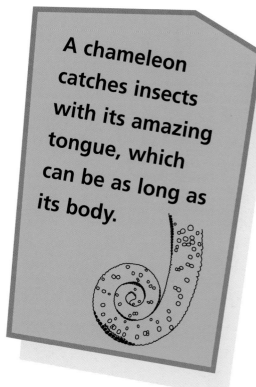

A chameleon catches insects with its amazing tongue, which can be as long as its body.

When I am full-grown I can weigh more than a small car. I use my large spoon-shaped tail to swim slowly through the water as I search for my favorite food, underwater plants and grasses. Because I am so big, I have to eat lots of plants every day— enough to fill a large refrigerator. Sometimes I eat all day long and don't stop until it's time to sleep.

Who am I?

I am a manatee. Some people call me a sea cow because I live in the ocean and eat plants like a cow. My home is in the warm waters around Florida in the southern United States. My life is usually slow, quiet, and peaceful, and I can live for 50 or 60 years, almost like humans.

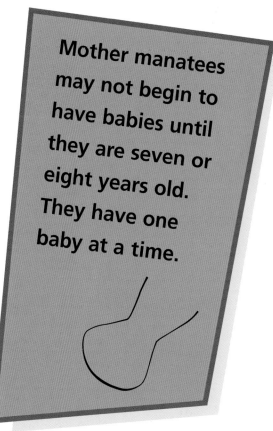

Mother manatees may not begin to have babies until they are seven or eight years old. They have one baby at a time.

When I am walking or running I often carry my long, striped tail high above my back like a flag. I live in groups with other animals like myself. There can be 25 of us in one gang with the oldest mothers in charge. During the day we climb around in trees searching for fruit, berries, young leaves, and insects.

Who am I?

I am a ring-tailed lemur and I live in the forests of Madagascar, just like the colorful chameleon you read about before. As you can probably tell from how I look, I am a close relative of the monkey. When I am young I stay close to my mother until I am almost half as big as she is. My favorite way to travel is to ride on my mother's back like a cowboy on a horse.

A giant snake is one of the most dangerous enemies of the ring-tailed lemur.

Index